W9-CQK-813

NEW FORMS
NEW
SPACES

NEW
FORMS
NEW
SPACES

BY

TOBY LURIE

1971

JOURNEYS INTO LANGUAGE

SAN FRANCISCO

New Forms New Spaces is published by
JOURNEYS INTO LANGUAGE
576 Liberty Street
San Francisco, CA 94114

Design and illustration by Lucille Arneson
Printed by Edward Brothers, Inc., Ann Arbor,Michigan
Distributed by Book People, Inc.
2940 7th Street, Berkeley, CA 94710

The following poems were recorded by Toby Lurie in the album,
Word Music CMS 615, 14 Warren St., N.Y., N.Y.
"Conversation," "I," "Waltz," "One Boy has Died in the War,"
"Simple Logic," "Nonsense Makes Sense in a Senseless World,"
"Goodbye."

Printed in the United States of America

for my family
jan
mark
drew
lisa
who said yes
allowed me to become
this to happen

FOREWORD

Toby Lurie is in the great American tradition of inventors, magicians, innovators. He is not part of any literary clique or wave: he invents poems in his backyard, so to speak, and they possess the simplicity, popularity, ingenuity and efficiency of a Model T. His poems are strong, naive, evocative; <u>social</u>, in that they bring people together, and ignore the differences and isolation of individuals in favour of a kind of family feeling for the rest of the race.

There is, however, a tough and exacting technique behind Lurie's work. Though some elements of what he does resemble European poésie concrète, his ingenuity is practical and American: his theory is not based on critical abstractions but on his sense of what moves and delights people.

Lurie's training was musical, and he uses every ounce of it in his poetry. He has an extraordinary ear for rhythm, and in his poetry even commonplaces and clichés are lit by a kind of magic. His poetry should be <u>performed</u>; he scores his lines, and his lines are a score, not only in the sense that they are signs to a performer, but also the rubric of a ritual happening.

I have heard him read several times, and every time a strange emotional pressure begins to build up as the reading progresses. One has to fight to keep one's detachment; one becomes aware of the faces and hands of one's fellowlisteners. Lurie's poems are sentimental but they are unabashedly and genuinely so. Lurie leaves nothing hidden: he brings out the excruciating nuances in the relation between father and son, man and wife. The people in his poems are not special, except that they are people: they are not particularly intelligent or learned, nor do they possess any special powers, like poor people or primitives gilded by a Marxist romanticism. Lurie's people are trying to get to grips with their lives, and there is no cheap satire on them, as from a superior, aristocratic or intellectual viewpoint. To do what he does takes courage: and his own life has been one of courage. He gave up a profitable business some years ago, and makes his living by reading his poetry all over the country. His poetry has a kind of dignity, a dignity of nakedness. He repeats a single word again and again with different emphases and musical rhythms, until it loses its meaning and breaks up into powerfully-loaded syllables, mutates into different words. He is a master of auditory illusion; he gets between our normal feedback rhythms and expected gestalts, and assaults our preconceptions. He is not embarrassed about following up the sort of mental tics that produce infinite regressions such as:

'. . .I realize my world contains:
My world containing your world, our world and my world,
Your world containing my world our world and your world and
Our world containing our world, your world and my world. . .'

Even when such things are cumbersome to say, we do think them and they are important: what I think you think I think, and even what you think I think you think I think, are important factors in a relationship. Perhaps the duration of our awareness is itself an infinite regression, a continual self-inclusion, a continuously growing set of all sets. Lurie tends to make fun of this kind of introspection (as in his titles: 'Simple Logic'; 'Psych I') but he recognizes with a sort of lucid frankness how much a part of our normal thinking it is, and he comes on odd profundities in the course of his description of it.

Lurie is something of a cult among college students, and it is part of his humility that he has allowed himself to become so. Like Dylan Thomas, he refuses to make himself inaccessible, forbidding, classic, esoteric. He has the same contempt for artistic poses as William Blake, the same slightly gaga quality, the same prophetic voice, the same middle-class peculiarities, the same commonsense and decency. The poetry of Toby Lurie is in my view an important phenomenon: it is a symptom and cause of the gradual movement one can see in this century toward a re-integration of art with the uses and passions of the real world.

Frederick Turner
University of California
at Santa Barbara

PREFACE

Here are a variety of poems
in a variety of forms
that represent my search
for a language.

I'm looking for a language
that will really work
as an instrument
for communicating feelings.

Feelings is an important word
in my world of language.
Feelings come from the inside,
language from the outside.

I would like to bring the two
closer together.
Barriers words place
around feelings
must be removed.

Words must express their
inner essence,
must be allowed to live.
They are organic, and
rhythm is their heartbeat.

Much of my poetry is scored
with the materials of music.
This gives special dynamics,
energy and color to words.

I've become aware of the
importance of space (silence)
as an element of poetry.
It gives words a chance

to stretch

                    and breathe

and what exists as space

between   words

is often more important

than what is said

between

                    the spaces.

It's difficult capturing some of
my poems on paper because many
of them have turned into outlines
which change at every reading.

This is a sort of rebirth
that pleases me.
No two moments are the same,
and I would like my work
to live in the present.

For those interested in learning the musical notations I have included a
Chart of Values. If not, just receive them in the way that's most com-
fortable. I'm only cranking up the engine so it can come to life. When
this happens take my poetry and let it become yours, infusing it with
your feelings, but PLEASE READ IT ALOUD. This is the only way that
language can be fully felt.

CONTENTS

CHART OF MUSICAL VALUES

Most of the poems in Parts 1 & 3 are scored with musical notations. This is for the purpose of expressing the colors, rhythms and dynamics of language. For simplification I will work with the basic unit of one beat, and relate it to the various units of sound and silence.

	Sound		Silence (rests)
1 pulse or beat	= $/$	=	ξ
1/2 pulse or beat	= Λ	=	7
1/4 pulse or beat	= F	=	$\exists$
1/8 pulse or beat	= F	=	$\exists$

1. When 1/2, 1/4, or 1/8 beats are adjacent they may be separate or connected by a straight line at the top.

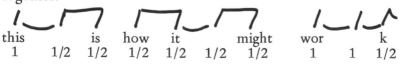

    this   is how it might work (or) this is how it might work

2. These sound pulses can be intermingled with rests as follows:

$1 = 1/2 + 1/2 = 1/4 + 1/4 + 1/2 = 1/2 + 1/4 + 1/4 =$

$1/4 + 1/4 + 1/4 + 1/4 = 1/4 + 1/2 + 1/4$

3. A dot (·) added to either sound or silence increases its duration by 1/2 its original value.

    $1 + 1/2$ $1/2 + 1/4$ $1/2 + 1/4$

4. When a curving line ⏝ connects two values it means to add them together.

    this   is how it   might wor   k

    1   1/2 1/2 1/2 1/2 1/2 1/2 1   1   1/2

5. Triplets are three pulses (sound or silence) of equal value, usually occuring within a period of one beat. They are generally connected by a broken bracket on top with a number three written between.

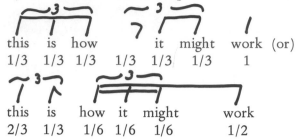

this is how   it might work (or)
1/3 1/3 1/3   1/3 1/3 1/3   1

this is how it might   work
2/3 1/3 1/6 1/6 1/6   1/2

6. The dynamic markings I have used are few and simple.

pp	= very soft	cresc.	= increase the sound
p	= moderately soft	dim.	= decrease the sound
f	= moderately loud	pitch up	= raise the pitch
ff	= very loud	pitch down	= lower the pitch

A wavering line ﹏﹏✗ following a pitch up, or pitch down direction indicates the pitch shall continue to rise or fall. An (x) at the end indicates a termination of direction.

⌢⸱ extend time pulse   rit: = slow the pace
⁊   accent sound   (·) = staccato

The basic principles of musical notation cannot possibly be condensed into such limited space, but this will be a helpful guide, and along with the natural rhythms of words and their arrangement on the page, the general feeling will come through.

I

WORDS
AND
MUSIC

L.ARNESON

DEAR MA DEAR DAD

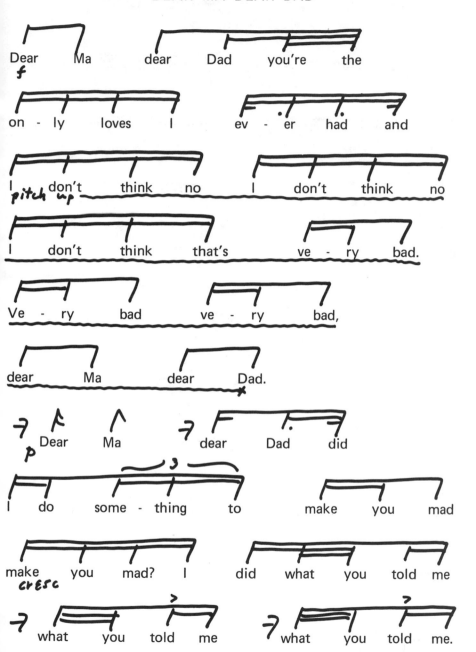

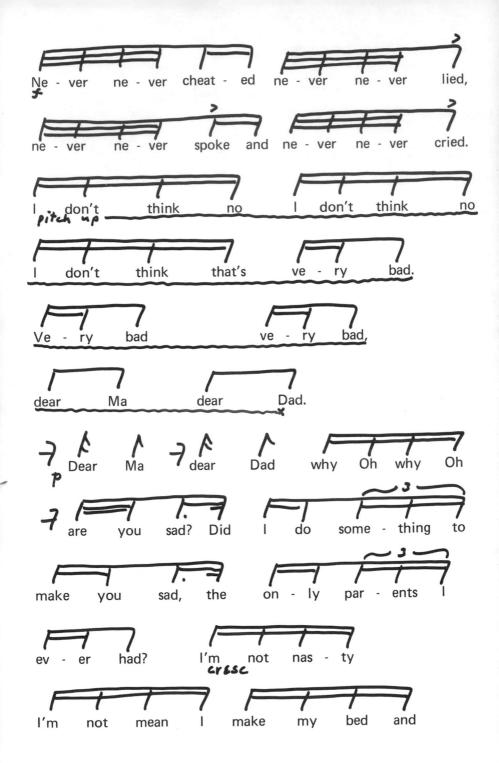

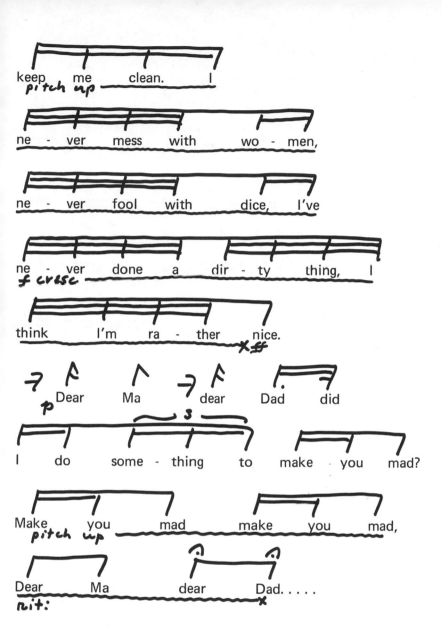

keep me clean. I
pitch up ————

ne - ver mess with wo - men,

ne - ver fool with dice, I've

ne - ver done a dir - ty thing, I
f cresc ————

think I'm ra - ther nice. *×ff*

p Dear Ma dear Dad did

3
I do some - thing to make you mad?

Make you mad make you mad,
pitch up ————

Dear Ma dear Dad. . . . .
rit:

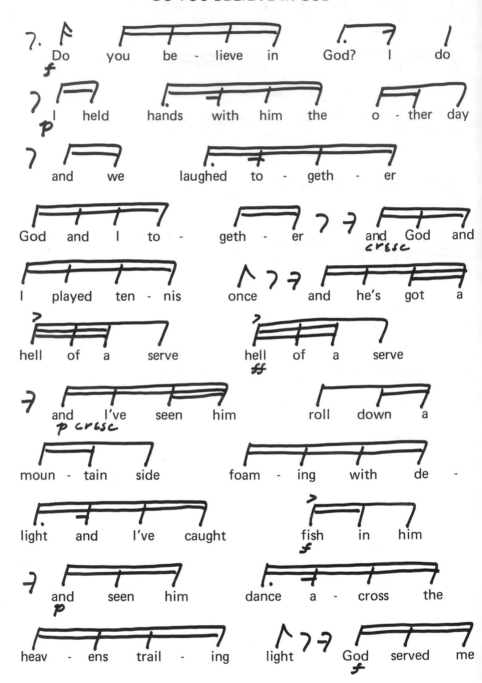

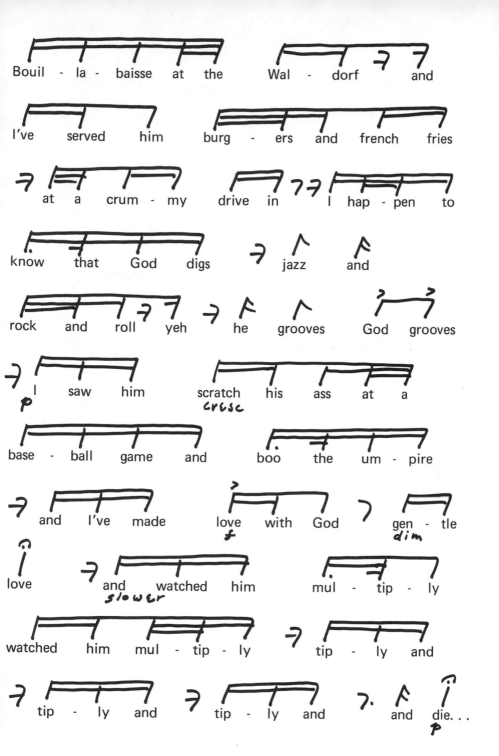

DREAMS

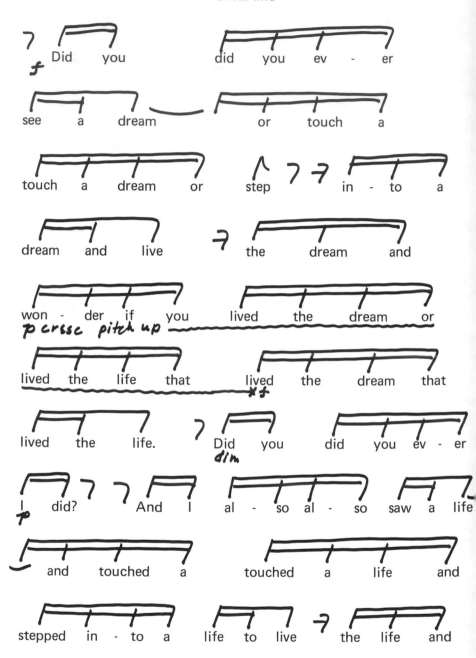

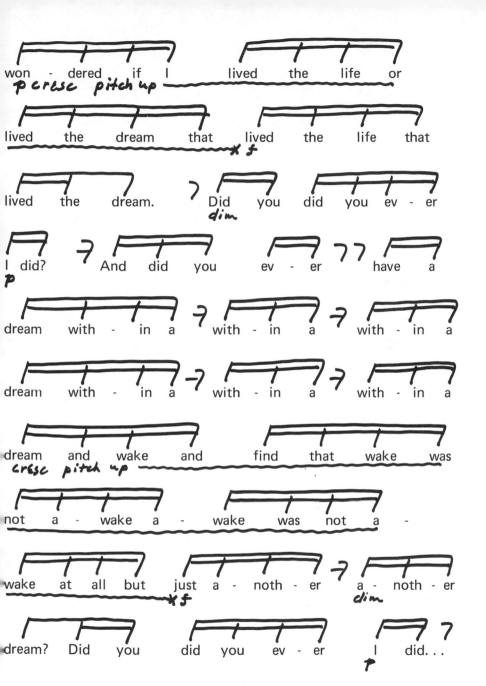

LIVE IT

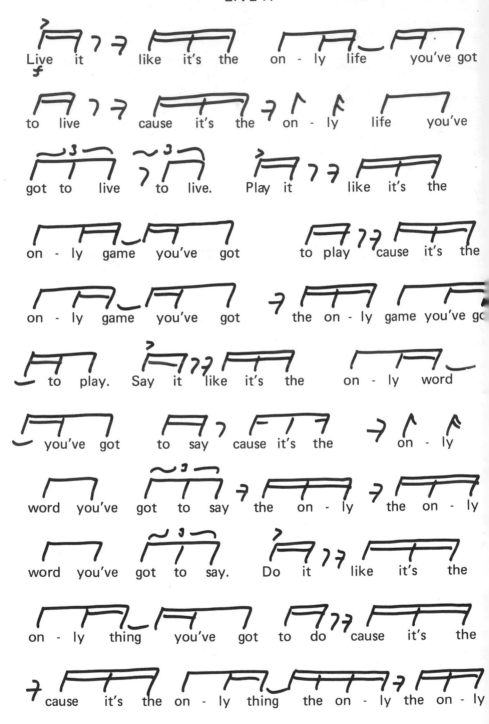

Live it like it's the on - ly life you've got

to live cause it's the on - ly life you've

got to live to live. Play it like it's the

on - ly game you've got to play cause it's the

on - ly game you've got the on - ly game you've go

to play. Say it like it's the on - ly word

you've got to say cause it's the on - ly

word you've got to say the on - ly the on - ly

word you've got to say. Do it like it's the

on - ly thing you've got to do cause it's the

cause it's the on - ly thing the on - ly the on - ly

hing you've got to do the on - ly word you've got
to say the on - ly game you've got to play
the on - ly life you've got the on - ly life you've got
dim
to live the on - ly life you've got to live the
on - ly life you've got to live the on - ly life
you've got to live the on - ly life you've got
to live to live the on - ly life to live
o live the on - ly life the on - ly life to live
to live to live to live
p *dim*
to live to live
live so live.
pp
p

NONSENSE MAKES SENSE IN A SENSELESS WORLD

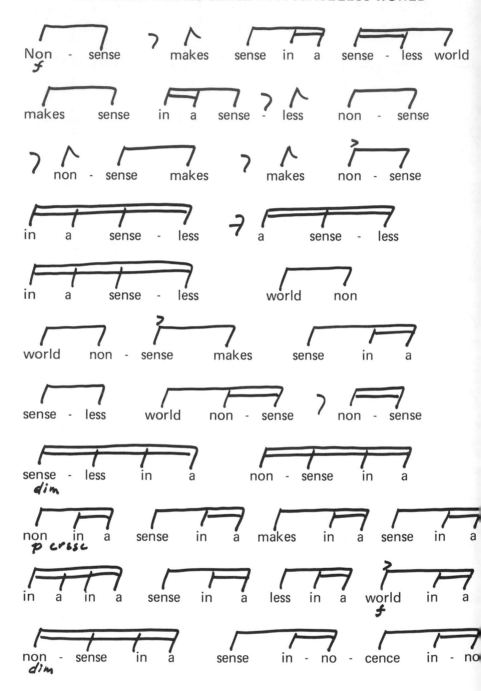

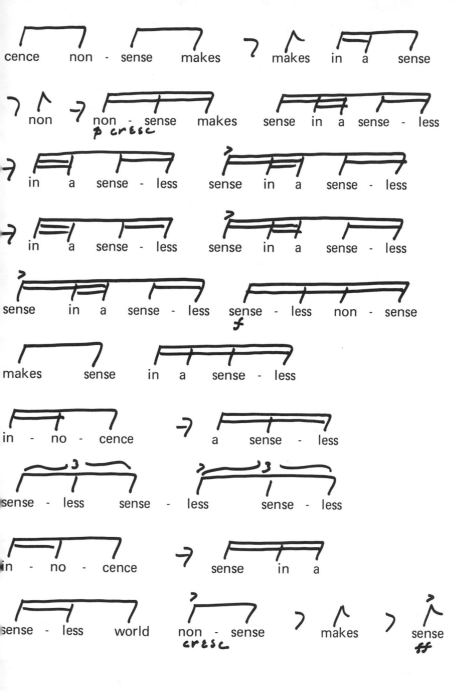

SIMPLE LOGIC

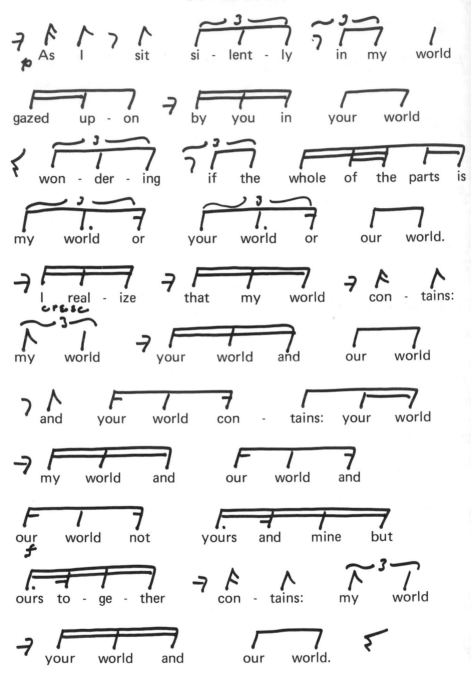

As I sit silently in my world
gazed up - on by you in your world
won - der - ing if the whole of the parts is
my world or your world or our world.
I real - ize that my world con - tains:
my world your world and our world
and your world con - tains: your world
my world and our world and
our world not yours and mine but
ours to - ge - ther con - tains: my world
your world and our world.

28

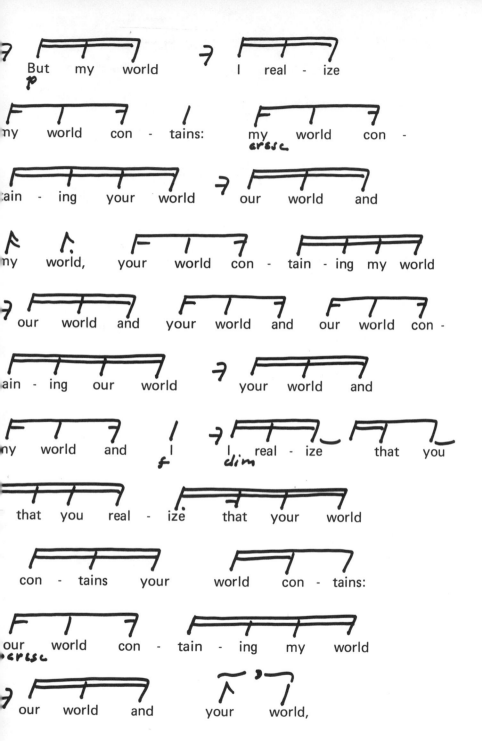

But my world   I real - ize

p

my world con - tains: my world con -

cresc

ain - ing your world   our world and

my world,   your world con - tain - ing my world

our world and your world and our world con -

ain - ing our world   your world and

my world and   I   I real - ize that you

f   *dim*

that you real - ize that your world

con - tains your world con - tains:

our world con - tain - ing my world

cresc

our world and   your world,

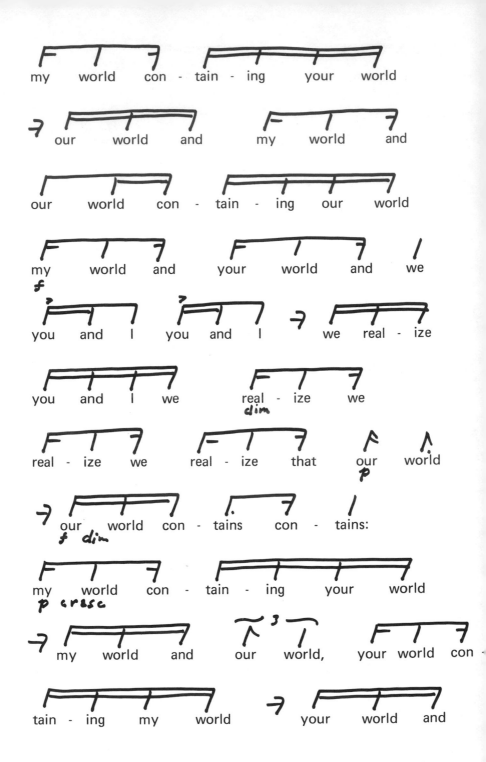

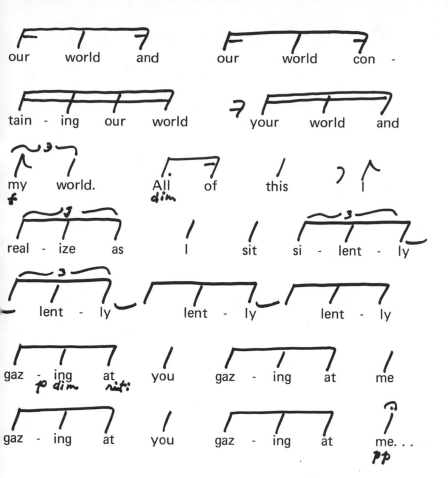

31

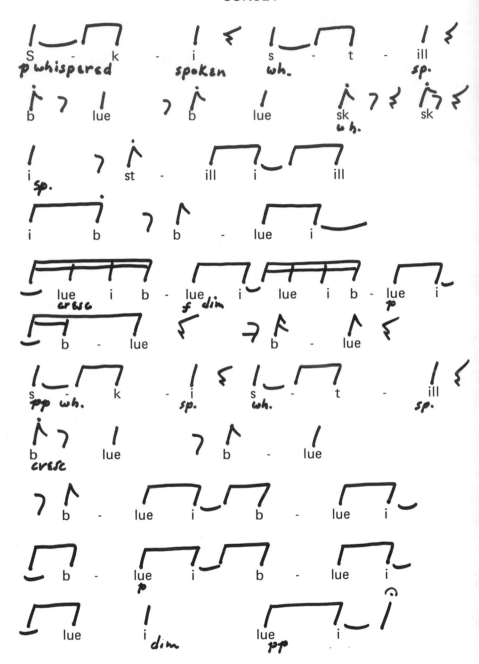

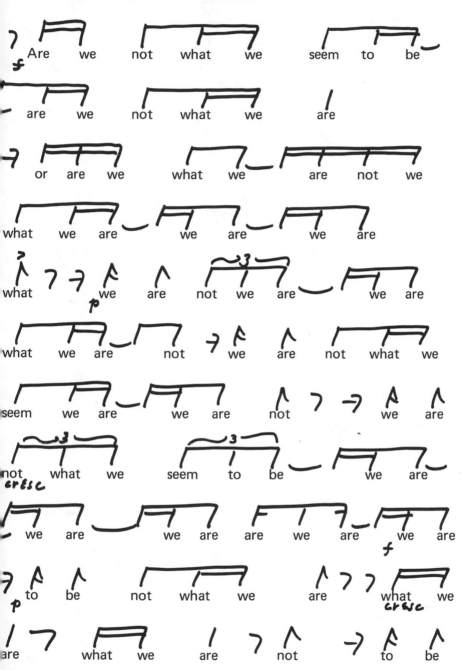

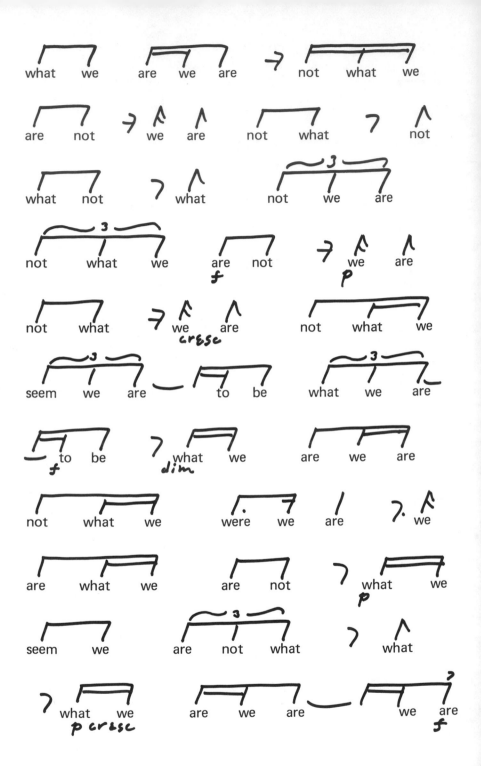

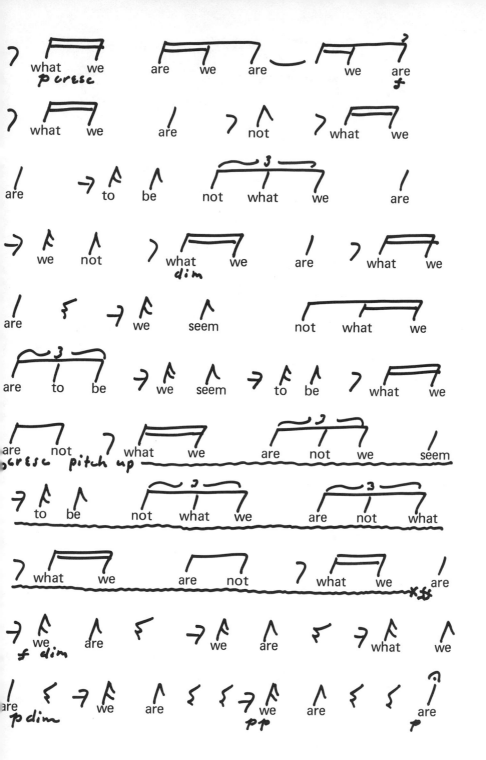

35

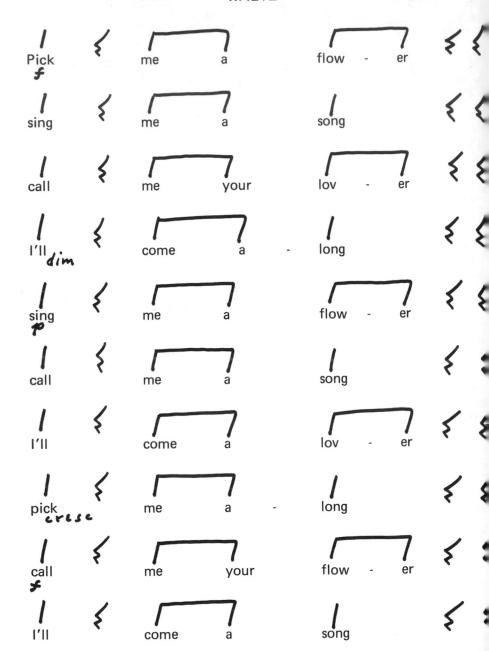

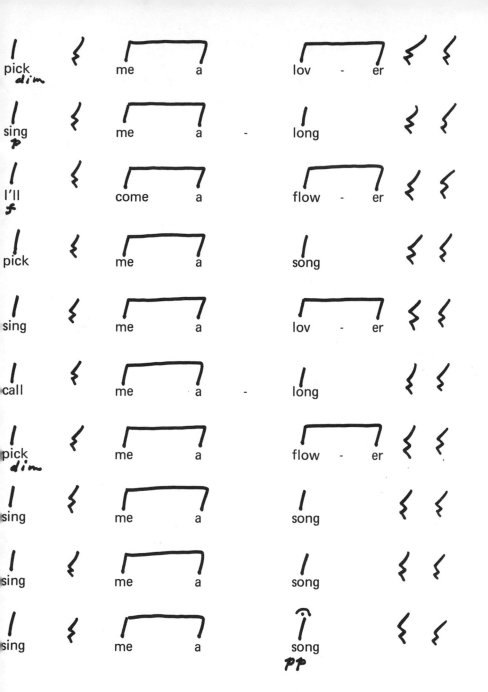

ONE BOY HAS DIED IN THE WAR

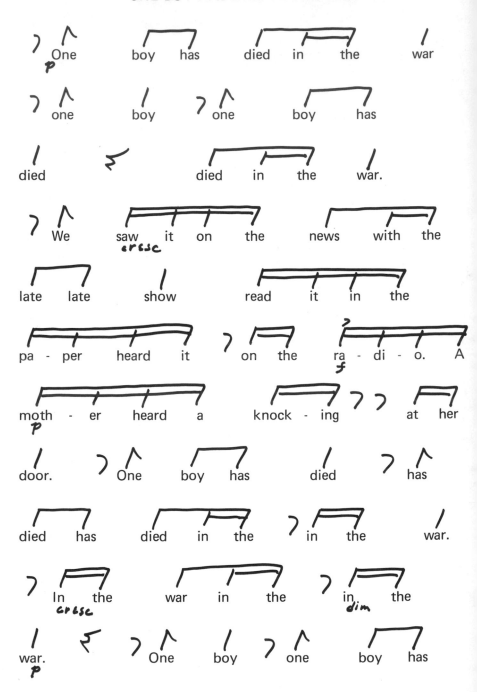

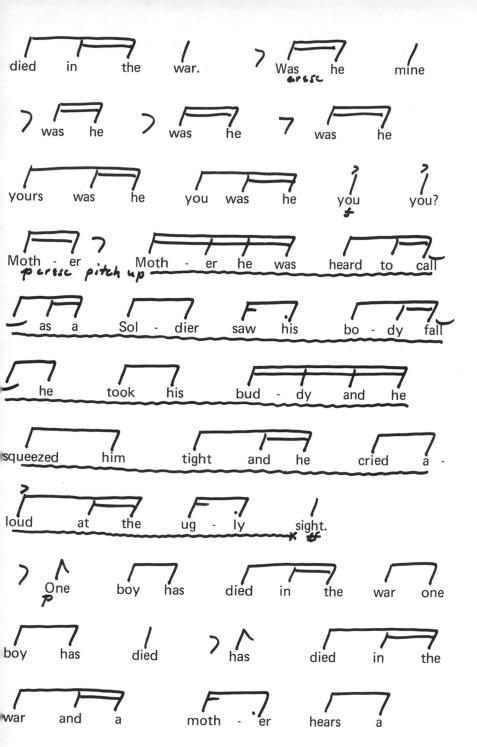

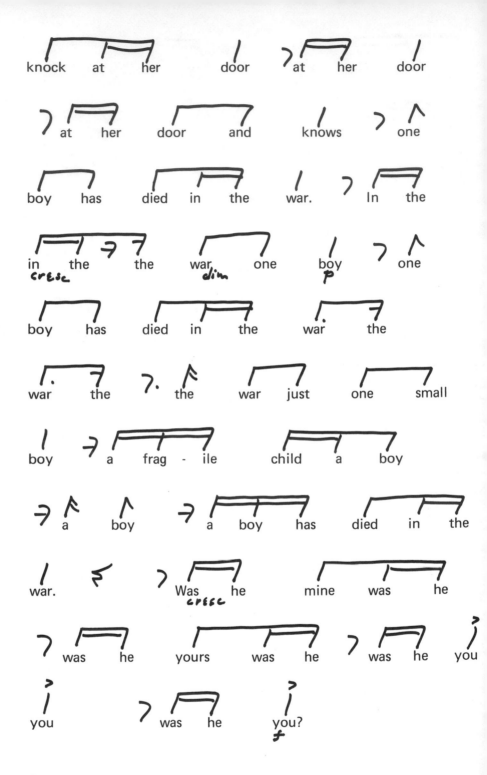

knock at her door door at her door

at her door and knows one

boy has died in the war. In the

in the the war one boy one
cresc dim p

boy has died in the war the

war the the war just one small

boy a frag - ile child a boy

a boy a boy has died in the

war. Was he mine was he
cresc

was he yours was he was he you

you was he you?
f

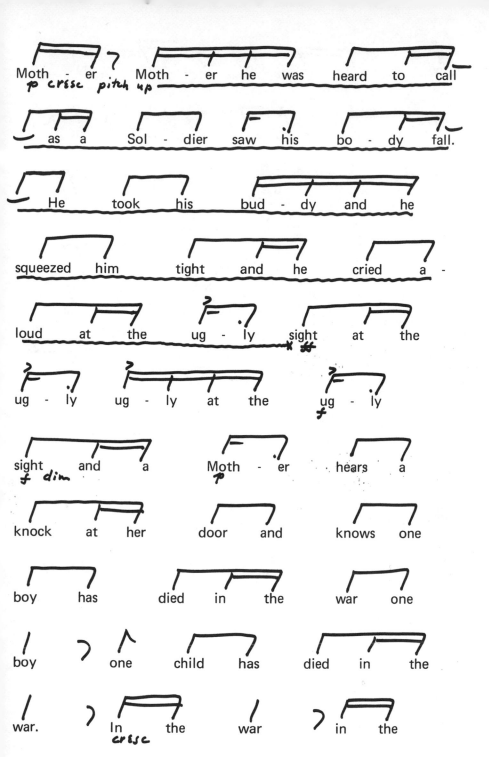

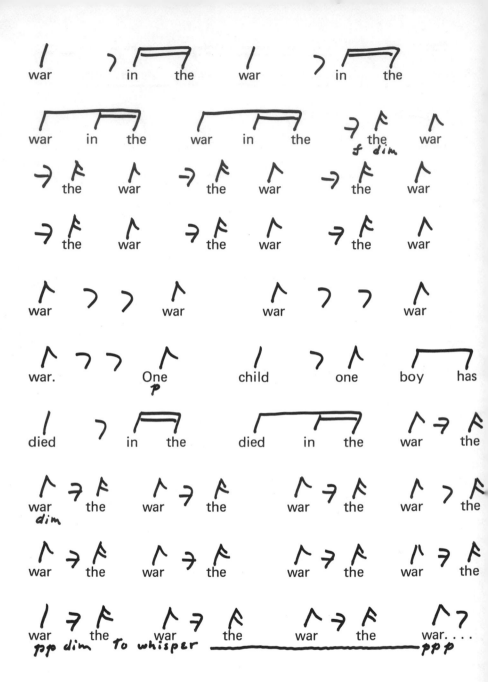

WELCOME TO MY MOST LONGING HEART

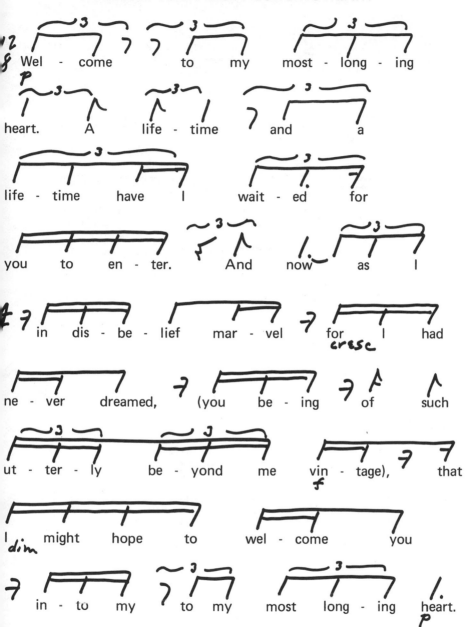

CLIMB ON

Climb on *p* climb on on on

climb on on on

dis - rupt the a - go - ny of my *cresc.*

va - cant mind va - cant

heart va - cant soul *f*

climb on on *dim.*

bless - ed one *p*

GOODBY

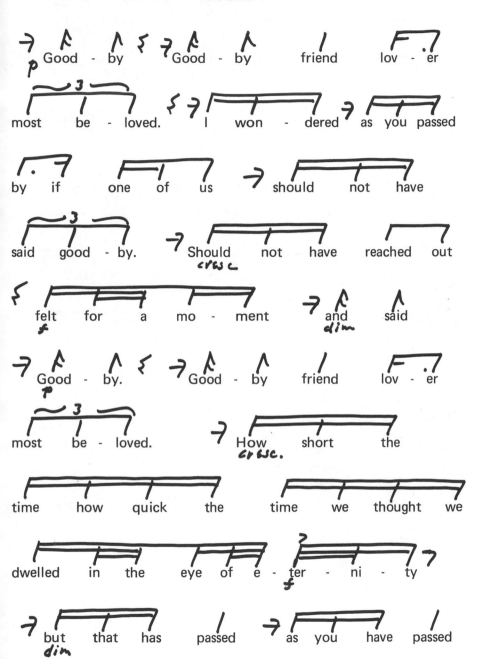

Good - by Good - by friend lov - er
most be - loved. I won - dered as you passed
by if one of us should not have
said good - by. Should not have reached out
felt for a mo - ment and said
Good - by. Good - by friend lov - er
most be - loved. How short the
time how quick the time we thought we
dwelled in the eye of e - ter - ni - ty
but that has passed as you have passed

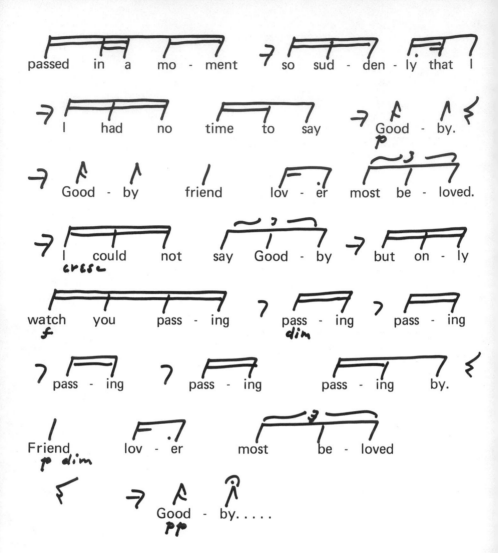

passed in a mo - ment ⇗ so sud - den - ly that I

⇗ I had no time to say ⇗ Good - by.
p

⇗ Good - by friend lov - er most be - loved.

⇗ I could not say Good - by ⇗ but on - ly
cresc

watch you pass - ing ⇗ pass - ing ⇗ pass - ing
f *dim*

⇗ pass - ing ⇗ pass - ing pass - ing by.

Friend lov - er most be - loved
p dim

⇗ Good - by. . . . .
pp

II

WORDS
ALONE

V. ARNESON

SUCCESS & FAILURE

I have succeeded in failing
for I have failed to succeed.

By failing to fail
I would have succeeded
in being successful.

If I am a successful failure
I have succeeded
by failing to succeed.

But if I have been
unsuccessful in failing
then I am an unsuccessful success.

If as a failure
I fail to fail
then I have failed again,
and can only hope to succeed
by failing to unsuccessfully fail.

Such success
can only lead to failure.

(A)
Some of my best friends are
some of my best friends

(B)
I don't give a damn what color you are
so long as it washes off

(A)
Of my best friends are
some of my best friends some

(C)
What color you are so long
as it washes off I don't give a damn

(A)
My best friends are some
of my best friends some

(D)
You are so long as it washes off
I don't give a damn what color

(A)
Best friends are some of
my best friends some of

(E)
I give a damn what color you are
so long as it don't washes off

(A)

My best friends are	some of my best friends	of my best friends
my best friends	best friends	friends

THERE IS TIME

There is time
there is still time
time for the undone to be done

there is time
there is still time
time for the undone to be done
time for the tear to be cried

there is time
there is still time
time for the undone to be done
time for the tear to be cried
time for what needs to be said
                  to be said

Yes there is time
yes   still time
time for the undone to be done
time for the tear to be cried
time for what needs to be said
                  to be said
time for what needs to be felt
                  to be felt

Yes yes there is time
but not much time
time for the undone to be done
time for the tear to be cried
time for what needs to be said
                  to be said
time for what needs to be felt
                  to be felt
time for what needs to be lived
                  to be lived

Yes there is time
a little time
but hurry
hurry

YOU

YOU   I'll never see you again

YOU   I may never think of you again

YOU   .   (whom I might have spoken to
                                       whom I might have touched
                                       whom I might have loved),

will grow old

          wither

                    die

                              before we even

                                        have a chance

to say   hello.

ROCKS

Today

        barefoot on the rocks

                        at Kern River

flat

round

angular

jagged

some beneath the surface

                       mossed and slimy

waiting for a victim

               and I

moving with the speed of certainty

laughing

knowing

falling

in a random

c   h

      o   r

          e

            o

               g

                 r   a

                     p

                       h

                         y

I LOST MYSELF

I lost myself yesterday

                or the day before.

Pages of myself neatly collected

with ideas

          and names

              and places

                    and dates

                        and poetry.

I'm somewhere out there

              between

Los Angeles   and   Santa Barbara.

I'd like to be a possession to someone

who hasn't found my name,

so can't return me.

                    I'd like that person

to study   and love

some of me,

          and maybe grow a little

                  from the mulch.

ME AT A ROAD

I waved at him

                              he waved back

I waved at her

                              she waved back

I waved at them

                              they waved back

I waved at her

                              she waved back

I waved and waved

                              they waved and waved

I stuck out my thumb arched in a traditional manner
furtive

        eyes

                through

                    a

                        rear

                            view

                                mirror. . . . .

QUANTITIES AND QUALITIES

It's not the quantity   it's the quality
                                                         it's the quality

It's not the quantity
    not the quantity
                    of the quantity or
                        the quantity of   the quality

But the quantity of the quality is not the quality of the quantity
                    it's the quantity

It's not the quality   it's the quantity
                                    Unless
the quality of the quantity
is a quantity of the quality
                                    or a quantity of the quality
                                    is the quality of the quantity
Or the quality of the quality
is a product of the quantity
                                    or the quantity of the quantity
                                    is a product of the quality

The quality being affected by the quantity and the quantity being
                    affected by the quality

So the quality of a quantity of the quality is the quantity
of the quality the quality
of the quality   being a quantity of the quantity

It's not the quantity   it's the quality
                                                        it's the quality
                                                        it's the quality

of the quantity
of the quantity
of the quantity
                                                        of the quality

BEACH 4.7.71

I'm free

free at last.

Free from the stifling lies,

free from the enterprise.

I've got no credentials

no damn degree   I'm free.

I wore a contraceptive on my heart

for 20 years — 40 years, but I've jerked it off,

and now I'm free.

Free from the doubt,

free from the need,

free from myself,

free from the greed.

Medical science knows how to transplant organs.

I was born with a total transplant,

but I've finally found my own,

and now I'm free.

Oh God how good it feels

to be free   to be free   to be free

                         to be free   to be free

                                                  to be free.

Beach,
I missed you yesterday,
the day before,
and today from my
Orange butterfly
I see you in small pieces.

Yours is not the only upheaval.

My feet are leatherbound today
but flakes of you
still hold on.

You are so stable
so predictable,
yet never quite the same.

I used to think of you
as a virtuoso lover
or were you the loved,
no difference.

Today I am bound to structure:
Piano at a dance class,
speech therapy for a friend
escaped into aphasia,
County and City taxes,
another car,
Lisa at Anacapa on the Micheltorena side,
and home to empty house
wife departed for a while.

BEACH 4.13.71

I am at you early today
after saying all the wrong things
to my son.
Things I believed in as I spoke
and rejected as I heard.

Tractors are passing over
your throat
draping it
in a mechanized garland.

I am alone
except for a few
drop-outs dropt in.

You are becoming a dear friend,
but I am doing all the talking.

tuscon

saturday morning

barefoot on a gravel road

jagged mountains in perimeter

cactus in erection

wild creosote in yellow abundance

(jerry told me so)

tumbleweed straining at barbedwirefence

SOUTHERN ARIZONA LAW ENFORCEMENT INSTITUTE

pick-up trucks bound for

anywhere

crazyman running on silverbell avenue

train whistle

passing through tuscon

it'll be a hot day

REFLECTIONS RECORDED WHILE DRIVING, LOOKING,
AND SMELLING ON THE VENTURA FREEWAY, ENTERING
LOS ANGELES, CALIFORNIA AT THE MORNING RUSH
HOUR.

There was a mountain over there.

                              I saw it clearly last year
                              or was it the year before
                              or the year before.
And the sun has turned to blood.

There was a sea over there   I remember it.
The colors blue, green, emerald,
            sparkling orange from the moon.
My body became wet in that sea — deliciously cold.
I can hear you but I cannot see you sea.
                              I saw you clearly last year
                              or was it the year before
                              or the year before.

And the sun has turned to blood.

And there was a forest   I remember you forest.
Heavy, thick with colors and trees and streams
and sweet smells.
I walked in you forest
                  slept inside of you
my head and lungs were full of you.
But where are you now   what has become of you?
                              I saw you clearly last year
                              or was it the year before
                              or the year before.

And the sun has turned to blood
      the sun has turned to blood
         sun has turned to blood
            has turned to blood
               turned to blood
                  to blood
                  blood.

Gertrude Stein was a lady.
Gertrude Stein knew she was a lady.
A lady knew she was Gertrude Stein.
Gertrude Stein, a lady, knew the lady knew Gertrude
Stein was a lady.
She knew she knew, and Gertrude Stein was a lady.
A lady knew.
A lady knew she was a lady.
A lady knew she was a lady but wouldn't have known
if she wasn't.
If she wasn't she wouldn't have known.
She wouldn't have known Gertrude Stein was a lady.
She wouldn't have known Gertrude Stein wasn't a lady.
She wouldn't have known Gertrude Stein.
Gertrude Stein would have seen to that.
She wouldn't have known Gertrude Stein was a lady
who knew.
She wouldn't have known Gertrude Stein was a lady
who knew she was a lady.
A lady who knew what a lady was, or a lady is, or should be.
But Gertrude Stein was a lady.
A lady who knew what a lady was.
A lady who never was or needed to be because
she knew she was.
Gertrude Stein.
Gertrude Stein.
Gertrude Stein was.
Gertrude Stein was a lady.
Gertrude Stein was a lady who knew.
Gertrude Stein was a lady who knew she was.
Gertrude Stein was a lady who knew she was a lady.
Yes, Gertrude Stein was a lady.
A man's lady.
A woman's lady.
Gertrude Stein was a lady who knew she was a lady,
and Gertrude Stein didn't give a damn.

THINK

If you think

that I think

that I think

you think

that
this
is   .
a
put - on

then

what do

you think

I think

you think it is

I think it is

you think?

III

NEW FORMS NEW SPACES

This section contains a variety of forms and spaces including; color improvisations, conversations, vocal and visual concrete poetry, and one-word poems.

My Color Improvisations are experiments with the color that exists in sound. In this form I escape from words into more fundamental sounds. In the work for three voices the lines connected by brackets are read together, and each part should relate to the others as far as indicated entrances and exits are concerned. It is not important to sound the letters precisely, in fact, more important not to: just feel their shapes and translate them into sound. The work for one voice was improvised on a typewriter and is an exercise in creating random color-tones.

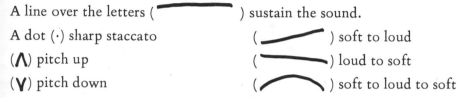

A line over the letters (⎯⎯⎯) sustain the sound.
A dot (·) sharp staccato   (⎯⎯⎯) soft to loud
(∧) pitch up   (⎯⎯⎯) loud to soft
(∨) pitch down   (⎯⎯⎯) soft to loud to soft

The poem, "Conversation," is a duet, and timing is important in the relationship between the parts. However, if the rhythms are too difficult, the general spacing between the voices will make it easier to read. This poem expresses the problem of our inability to communicate with each other as father and son go 'round and 'round, but never quite touch; never quite understand.

The Vocal and Visual concrete poems are a juxtaposition of the visual and the vocal elements of language. The visual is an ancient form of poetry. The vocal is new. Here it is not so important <u>what</u> is being said but <u>how</u> it is being said, so the dynamics of the language are vital. The poems "I", and "Oh Yes," should be read aloud, together, and perhaps combined with another feeling improvised from the moment. Like musicians improvising at a jam session, there is an interaction of ideas and moods that often produce surprising results.

One-word poems were developed from my interest in the organic quality of words. I am trying to crack words open and release the energies that exist within them. At first I performed these poems strictly as written, but when audiences became more involved these poems became improvisations with chanting, singing, dancing, and musical instruments. It is interesting to interlace these poems and allow them to discover each other. They can become real celebrations if you let yourself go, and allow yourself to become.

COLOR IMPROVISATION
for three voices

1) ooooooooolllllllllld ȧ ȧ ooooooooolllllllllld ȧ
2) rrrrrrrrrrrrrrrrrrrrrrt ṫ ṫ rrrrrrrrrrrrrrr

1) ẇ ẇ weeeeeeeeeeeeeeee ẇ ẇ weeeeeeeeee
2) ṫ ṫ ṫ ṫ
3) żżd żżd żżd żżd

1) ṗ ṗ ṗ ṗ ṗ
2) ṫ ṫ ṫ ṫ ṫ ṫ ṫ ṫ
3) żżd żżd żżd żżd

1) ṗ ōōōōōō ōōōōōōōōōōō
2) ṫ mmmmmmm
3) żżd żżd żżd

1) ǩ ǩ hōōōōōōōō hōōōōōōōō
2) mmmmmmmmmmmmmmm ṗ
3) zzdzzdzzdzzdzzdzzdzzdzzdzzd sssssssssssss

1) ōōōōōōōō hōōōōōōōōōōōōōōōṗ hōōōōōōōōōōōōṗ
2) ṗ ṗ ṗṗddṗ ṗṗddṗ ṗṗddddṗṗ
3) hhhhhhhcvcvcvbum cvcvcvcvbum bum

69

1)   quh   quh   quh

2)   ppd   ppd   ppd

3)   bum   bum   bum

1)   quh   quh   quh

2)   ppd   ppd   ppd

3) bum   bum   bum   bum   bum   bum   bum

1) iiiiiiiiiiiiissssssssssshhhhhhhhhh   lllllllllliiiiiiiivvbvvbvvbvvbvvb

2)   t   rrrrrrrrrrr   d   d   trrrrrrrr   d

3) bum   bum   bum   bum   bum   bum   bum

1) vvbvvbvvbvvbvvbvvbvvbvvbvvbvvbvvbvvbvvbvvbvvb   vv

2)   wd   wd   wd   wd   trrrrrrrrrrrrrrrrrrrrrd

3) bum   bum   bum   bum   bum   bum   bum

1) tyopldld   tyoplplp   ffeffeffeffeffeffeffeff

2)   kljhjkjlkjlkopopopopopopopwewewewewewewopweopwe

3) bum   bum   bum   bum   bum   bum   bum

1) efesdesdesdesdesdeskkioepgkwostswostsdfwgeujfhgjikikikikiksdsds

2) opweopweopweop   zzzzzzzzzzdddddddffffffooo

3) bum   bum   asssassssasss   asssssssssss

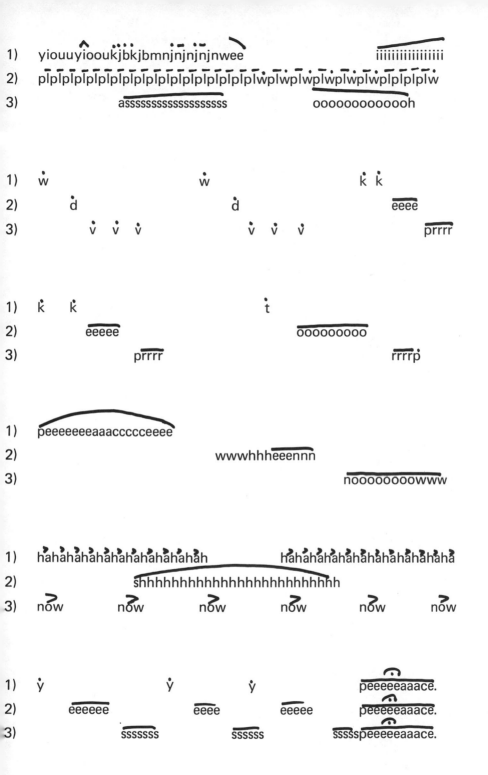

71

qwer tyUiop lkjhgfdsa fdsaaazs zsertgh

THPO TTTTTTeer eeeerrrp p p

LLLLLLLLp p p

p OOOOOHGGGGYYOWWOWOWO

bn bbn bbbn bbbbn nw nw nw

KKLPYTR kipokipo otkldffffubv WRPLKMJhnd

wdv wdv wdv

WDVWDVWDVWDVWDV

RTY rty

LPLLPLLLPLLPLP mmnmnmnw mnmnmnwp

OLKOLK KLJI KLLJI KLLLJ ytytytytytytytytyty

sdklweiuth p o i r sW H uSPOK u

kIPO HYDTeri ki koapwh WPOLKFU

hkhk jljlltjljlltllt t jlljlljlT

toooopooopr

ôôôôôôôôôôôôôôô

ZZZZZZZZZZZZZMP P P P

RRRRrrrr ejej iot iot iotp i o t p

wrt op

lkrrlkrr LKTRYW

K k P POO b

bmm lk lk l

In T N MKMKMKMKMKMKMKMKAH

AAAAAAAAAAAAAAAAAAAAHH
p clim ppp

CONVERSATION
(father & son)

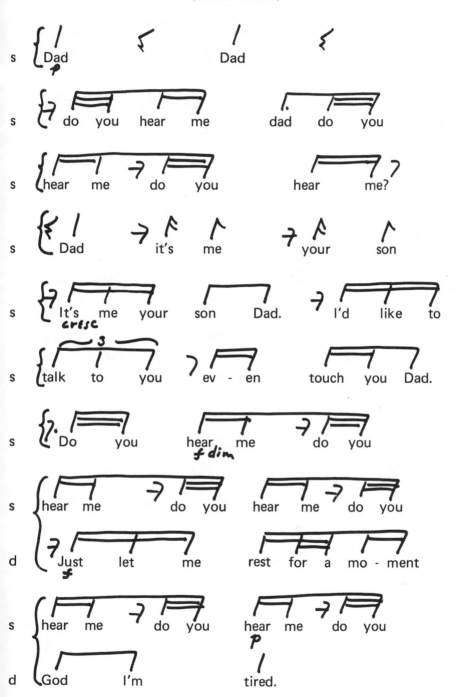

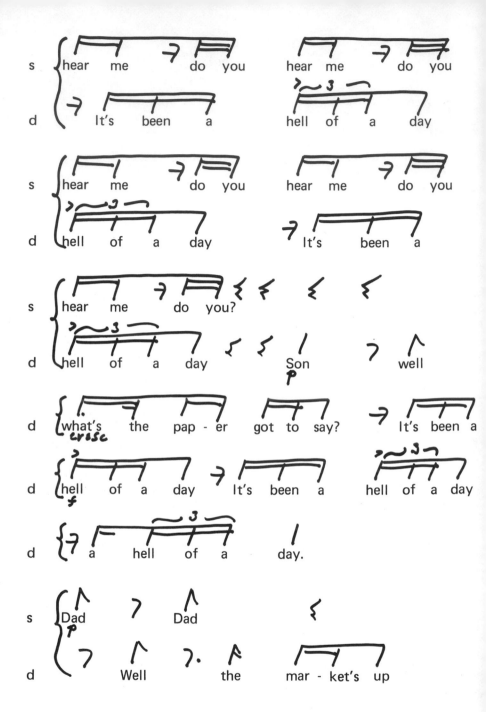

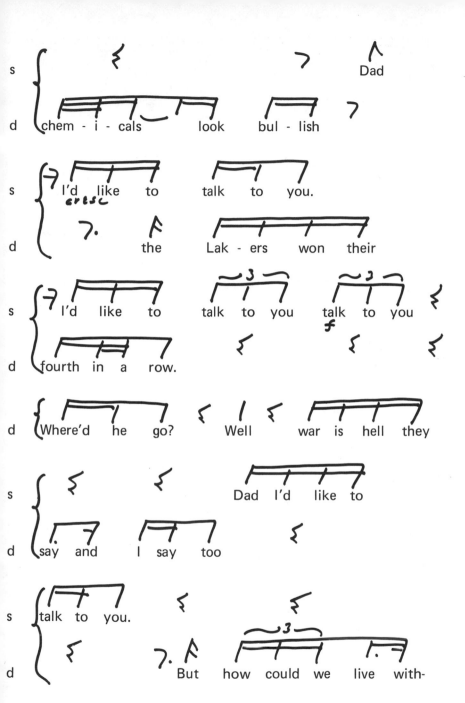

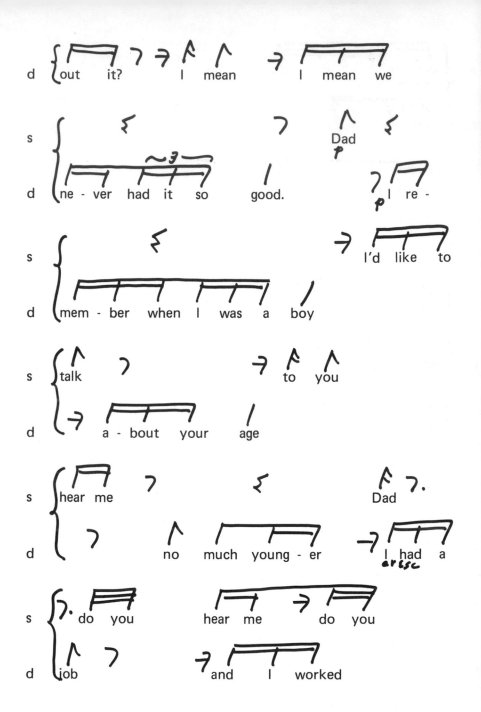

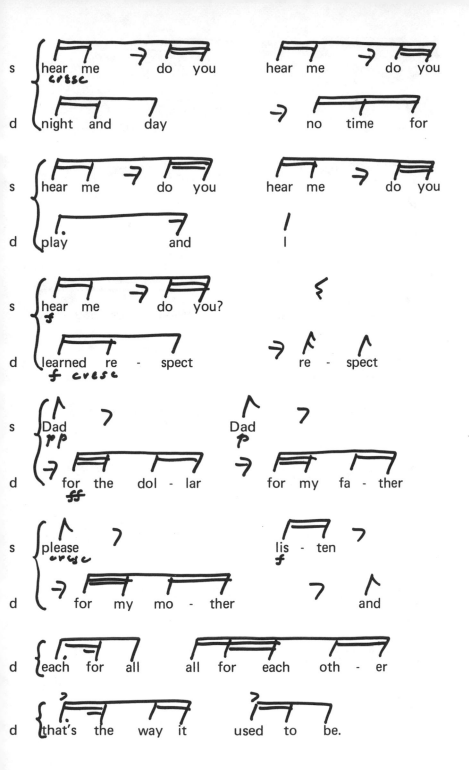

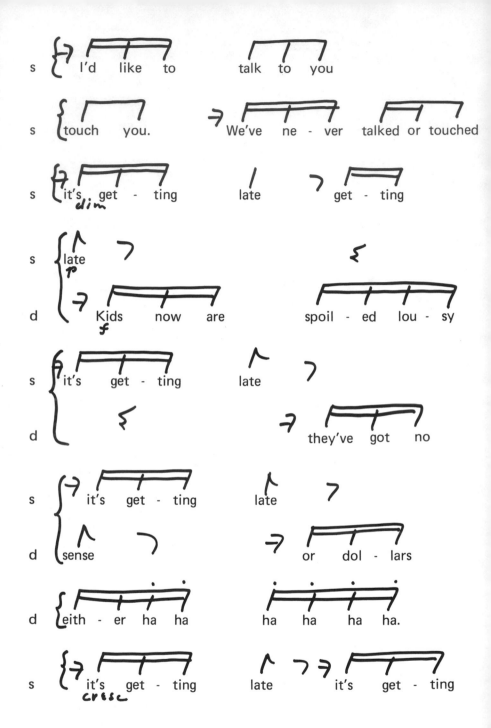

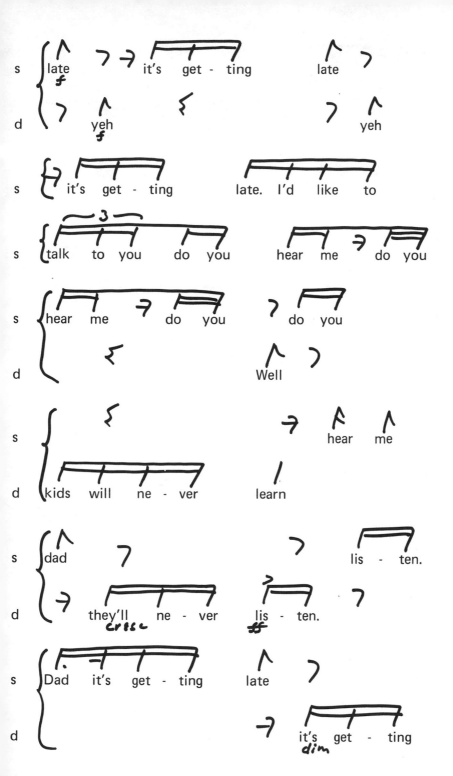

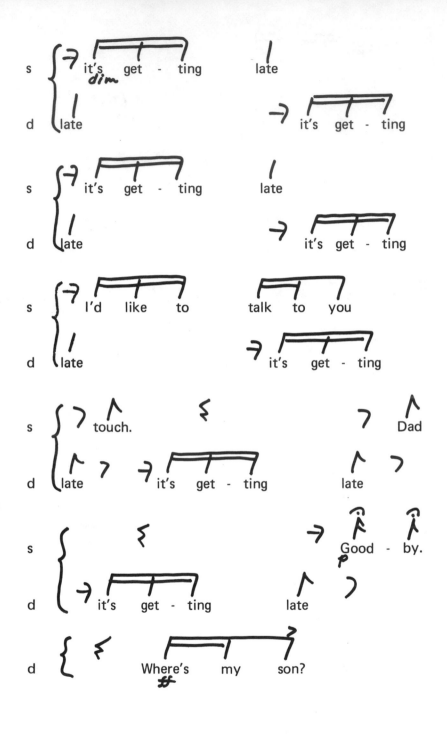

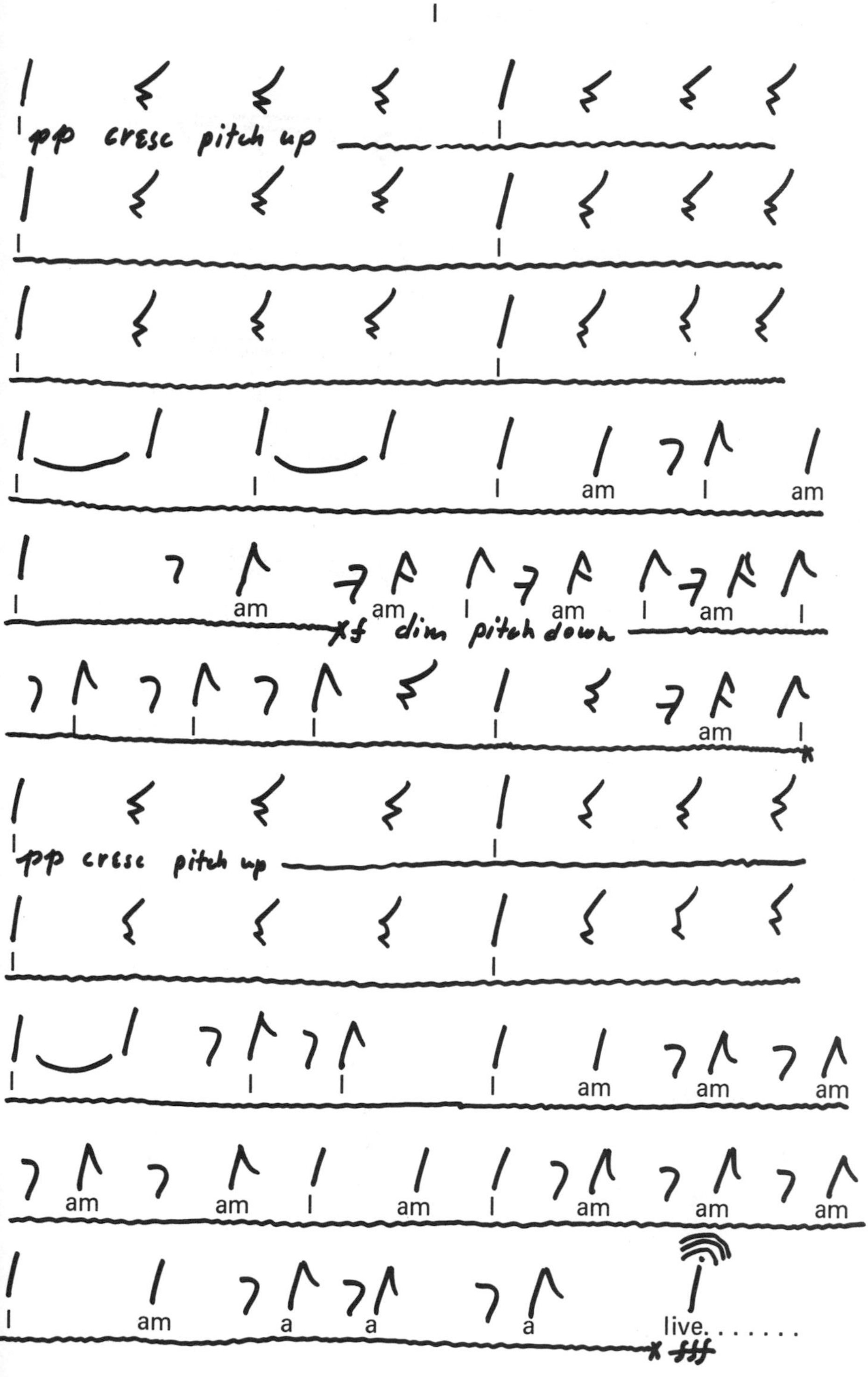
pp cresc pitch up
am
xf dim pitch down
pp cresc pitch up
a
live. . . . . . .
fff

HAPPENING # 6

yeeeeeeeeees   yeeeeeeeeeees   oooooooooh

yeeeeeeeeeeees   yeeeeeeeeeeeeees

oooooooooooooooooooooooooooooooooooooooooohhh   yeeeeeeeeeees

aaaaaaaaaaaaaaaaaaaaaaahhhhhhhhhhhh

yeeeeeeeeeeeees
yeeeeeeeeeeees
yeeeeeeeees
yeeeeeeeees
yeeeeeees
oh   GOD   YEEEES

YEEEEES

SHHHHHHHHHHhhhh
h
hhhhhhhh
hhhhhhhh
hhhhhhhhhh
yes   yes   yes   yes

hahahahahahahahahahahahahahahahahahahahahahah

aaaaaaaaaaaaaaaaaaaaaaaaaaaaaaaaaaaaaahhhhhh
yeeeees
yeeeeeees

ooooooooooooooooooooooooooooOOOOOOOOOOYESYESYES

shhhhhhhhhhhhhhhhhhhhhhhhhhhhhhhhhhhhhhhhhhhhhhhhhhhhhhhhhh

AVALANCHE

AVALANCHE

AVALANCH
      E

        C
AVA L   N   h
     A
            E

               N

    V   a
A
     a   I   C   h

                   E

     V
A
        I
    a   A
            C
A   N
  v v V   A   H E

        I L
          A a
             N
              C
               C
            H
          E
           E
            E E
              e
            e
           e
          e

```
              GODOGOD
              GODOGOD
              GODOGOD
              GODOGOD
              GODOGOD
              GODOGOD
GODOGODOGODOGODOGODOGODOGODOGODOGODOG
GODOGODOGODOGODOGODOGODOGODOGODOGODOG
GODOGODOGODOGODOGODOGODOGODOGODOGODOG
GODOGODOGODOGODOGODOGODOGODOGODOGODOG
              GODOGOD
              GODOGOD
              GODOGOD
              GODOGOD
              GODOGOD
              GODOGOD
              GODOGOD
              GODOGOD
              GODOGOD
              GODOGOD
              GODOGOD
              GODOGOD
              GODOGOD
              GODOGOD
              GODOGOD
              GODOGOD
              GODOGOD
              GODOGOD
              GODOGOD
              GODOGOD
              GODOGOD
```

MAMMALIAN COMPLEX

I   am   a   breast   man   I

   am   a   breast   man   I   I

      a   breast   man   I   I   am

         breast   man   I   I   am   a

            man   I   I   am   a   breast

               I   I   am   a   breast   man

               I   am   a   breast   man   I

               I   am   a   breast   man   I

               I   I   am   a   breast   man

           man   I   I   am   a   breast

       breast   man   I   I   am   a

     a   breast   man   I   I   am

   am   a   breast   man   I   I

I   am   a   breast   man   I

LIFE IS LIKE A TUBE OF TOOTHPASTE

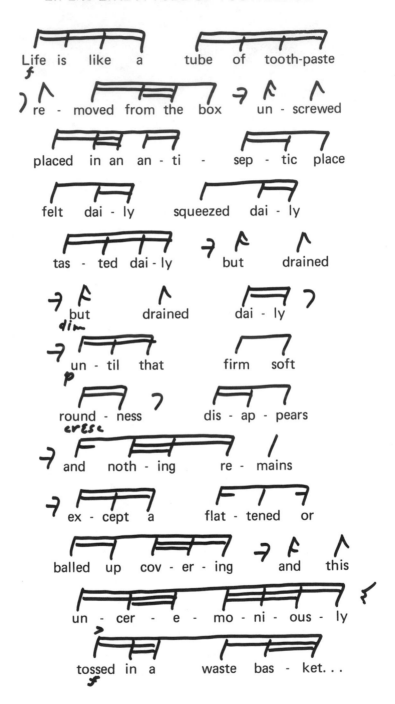

ORGY

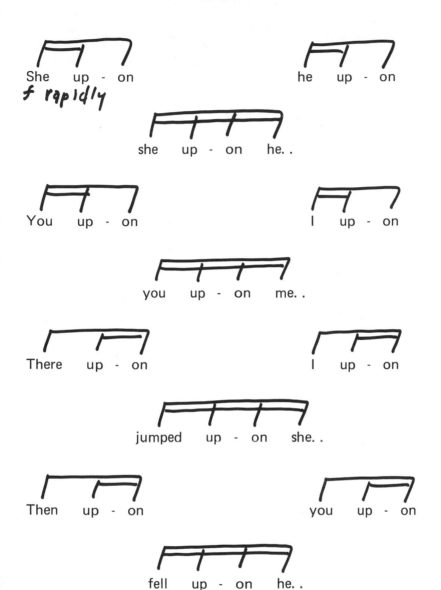

INNOCENCE

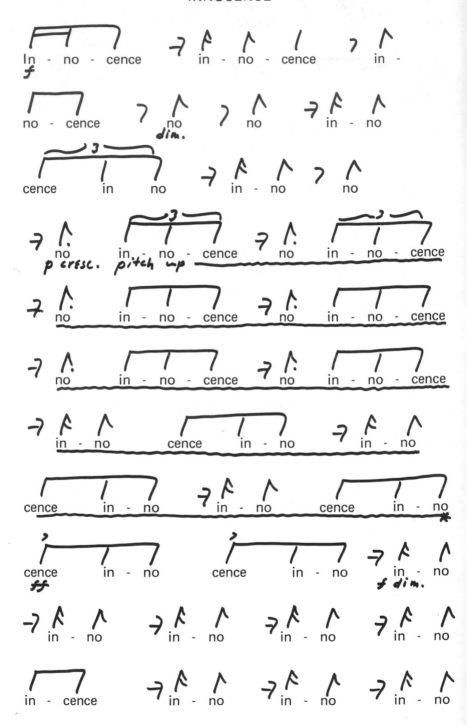

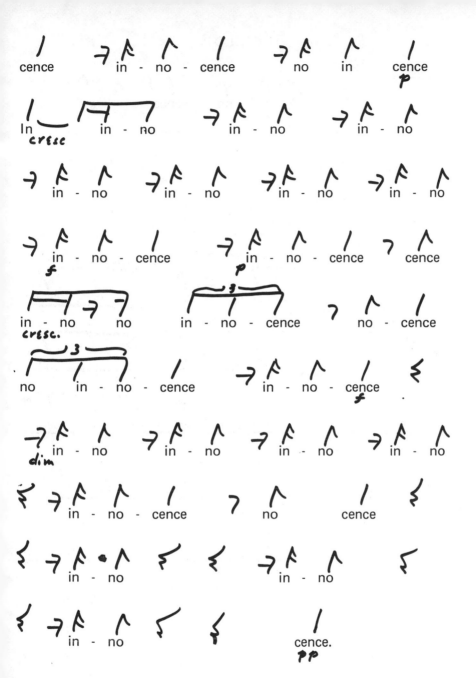

CHILD

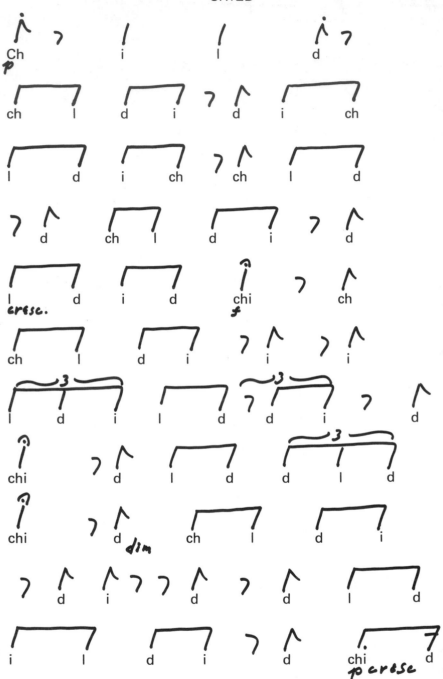

90

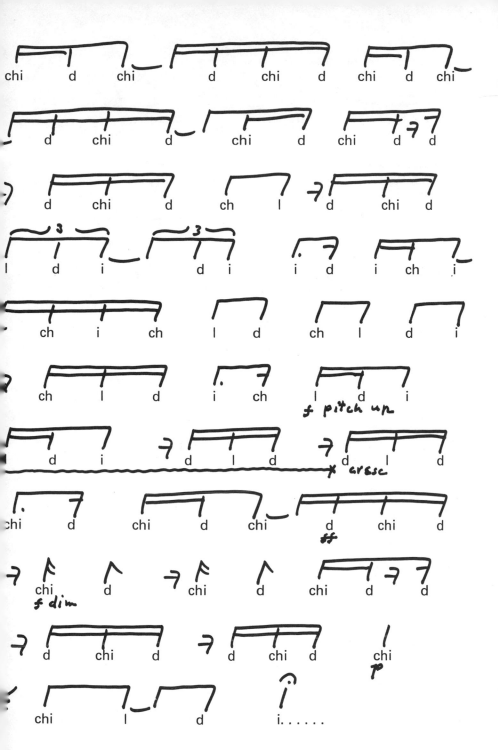

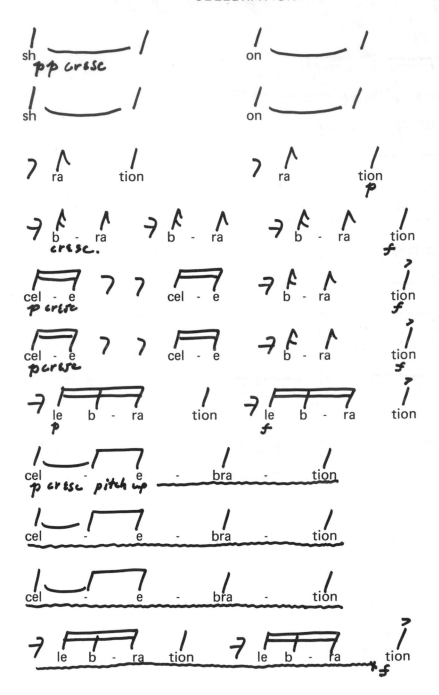

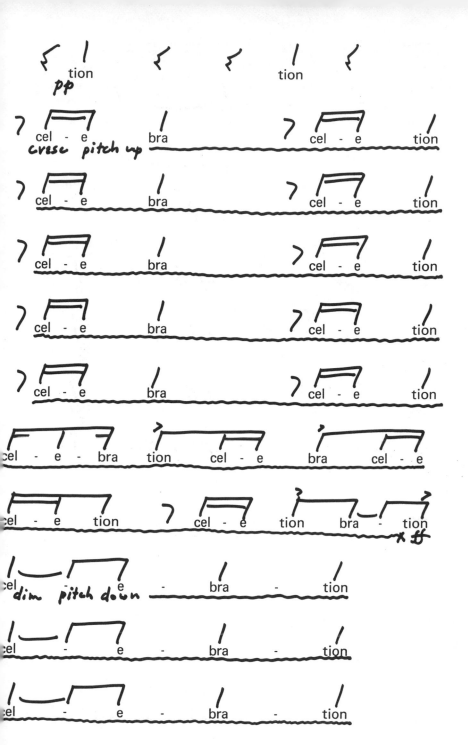

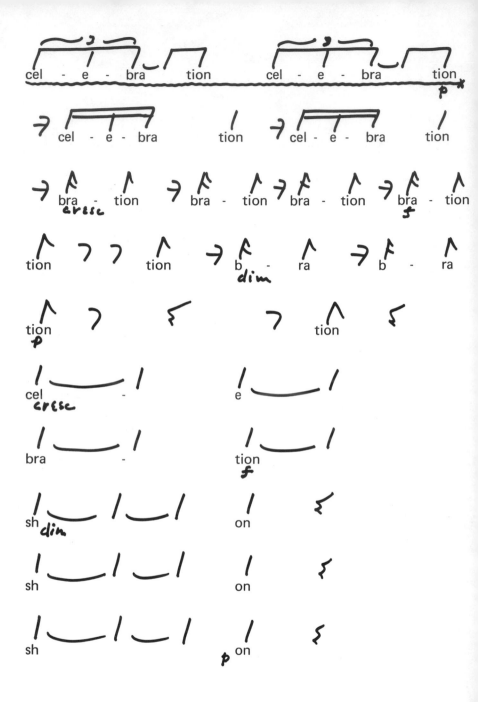

cel - e - bra tion   cel - e - bra tion

p

cel - e - bra   tion   cel - e - bra   tion

bra - tion   bra - tion   bra - tion   bra - tion

cresc   *f*

tion   tion   b - ra   b - ra

dim

tion   tion

p

cel   e

cresc

bra   tion

f

sh   on

dim

sh   on

sh   on

p

and on, and on, and on, and on, and on, and on, and on, and on,

PB_38412
5-40